A Girl and Her G🌻D

A Girl and God

Her GOD

Growing and Glowing in His Glory

SHANIQUA L. HOWELL

Dedication

To Rudolph Browne (Mr. X). Thank you for always believing in me, supporting me and encouraging me to become the best version of me. You came into my life at a young age and remained until your death. You are deeply missed and will forever be remembered.

Edited by: Jalisa Thomas
Edited by: Paula Richards - Eagle's Eye Editing Services
Email: eagleseyeservices@gmail.com

Cover Photo: @theoptimistdreamer from nappy.co
Cover Design: Shelev Publishing

SHELEV PUBLISHING
"Don't just dare to dream; live your dreams"
Email: Shelevpublishing@outlook.com
Telephone: 1 (246) 257-9611

At the back of this book is a journal specially laid out for you. It features various quotes/ poems from local ministers and poets. Additionally I did some of the pages without quotes, poems or scriptures so you can personalise your own journal entries with whatever you choose. May your pen connect to the paper and create something magical ☺

ISBN: 978-976-96117-3-3

Table of Contents

Introduction

Not all plants grow the same way; some grow from seeds and some plants use asexual vegetative reproduction and grow new plants from rhizomes or tubers. Whatever the case, they should always grow. A plant that does not grow is dead and useless.

If a plant has not grown since it was planted, one must check the plant's root system. Are you rooted securely in God? Perhaps the whirlwind is sweeping you up because your root system is terribly weak. Growing spiritually will sometimes happen in leaps and bounds, and other times our growth will tend to be a bit slower, but not growing at all is the problem. After years in the ground some of us have not even grown an inch; this is downright scary. You are being called higher; the glow up will be real if you will only choose to grow up. Will you make your relationship with God the priority in your life today?

Chapter 1

Reckless Love

"**I** know that I want to change; I want a better life for myself but I am chained to my past by the people around me. They hold me prisoner to who I was instead of seeing me for who I could be. Shame will forever be my shadow it seems, there is no escaping the stares, atrocious comments and loud laughter whenever I walk by. "Sinner!!" they shout. I am constantly burned by the fire of their words. Jesus is visiting the house of Simon the Pharisee, the very same man who taunts me without end. However, I need to see the Man everyone is talking about, Simon and his fellow accusers will not get into my head today, because without fail I am going to meet the One who could bring hope to my hurt. With sweaty palms, a speedily beating heart and a determined mind, I set out to meet my soon to be Lord. Maybe just once someone would see my heart instead of remembering me by my history." — ***The Sinful Woman***

Then one of the Pharisees asked Him to eat with him. And He went to the Pharisee's house, and sat down to eat. And behold, a woman in the city who was a sinner, when she knew that Jesus sat at the table in the Pharisee's house, brought an alabaster flask of fragrant oil, and stood at His feet behind Him weeping; and she began to wash His feet with her tears, and wiped them with the hair of her head; and she kissed His feet and anointed them with the fragrant oil. Now when the Pharisee who had invited Him saw this, he spoke to himself, saying, "This Man, if He were a prophet, would know who and what manner of woman this is who is touching Him, for she is a sinner." Luke 7:36-39

She was the woman with the box and a heart of gold; her story shows the true beauty of God's love and forgiveness. Everyone in town labelled her as the 'sinner'. Walking the streets each day would have been hard because of the judgmental and prideful Pharisees who always lie in wait, ready to call her out by her sin.

There comes a time in our lives when we have to discern and acknowledge our mistakes and make the choice to move on. The sinful woman decided she was not about to sit down in her filth for the rest of her life; she got up and went in search of someone who she presumed would make her life better. Despite knowing the cruelty she would experience upon entering Simon's house, she still pressed on to have that encounter with Jesus.

When she came to meet with Jesus she was not empty handed, for she carried an alabaster box filled with perfume. The contents of an alabaster box were usually so valuable that you weren't supposed to just use it on anyone. To bring the box to Jesus meant a whole lot that the people in the room could not understand. It was a sign of honour, surrender and great appreciation. Giving Him such an expensive box wasn't enough; she washed his feet with her tears while drying them with her hair. As she continued to honour Him, she kissed his feet and anointed them with the fragrant oil.

Everything about her screams humility and authenticity. She was not putting on a show like many other people around town when in the presence of Jesus. Well aware of her past decisions which left her with a stained identity, she was hungry for something new and was looking for love, acceptance and forgiveness. Words never came from her mouth, but her heart sang a song of repentance. She wept in his presence: tears of sorrow for her sins, tears of gratitude for His goodness and tears from the shame and scorn. Jesus welcomed her touch and never once pushed her away as the others would have done. He was marvelled by her, while others were probably mad at her for being in the same room as them.

One of the first steps in growing and glowing in the Lord is acknowledging your sinful state and making the decision to make a 180 degree turnaround. Perchance you have never accepted Christ into your heart or you have been a Christian for a long time but have now found yourself in a backslidden state. Know that forgiveness is free, but you have a part to play. She was extremely desperate for what Jesus could offer that she went into the house among the very people who taunted her day in and day out. Are you desperate? Have you come to the place where you are tired and fed up of the life you are living? It is time for you to break your alabaster box in the presence of God.

Simon had seen enough. "Isn't that the old dirty sinner from down the road, why would she even show her face among us? This is unacceptable!" he most likely thought.

Everyone in the room was staring at Simon for his response to what was happening; he needed to make an example out of her and quickly, they probably reasoned.

"If he were truly a prophet he would know what type of woman was touching him," Simon grumbled to himself.

Watch mercy, grace, love and forgiveness at their finest; Jesus perceived Simon's thoughts and stood up on her behalf. The 'sinner' as they would call her was nothing but scum to them. However, she was way much more than that to Him who welcomed her, and He was not about to let them degrade her in His presence.

> *Then He turned to the woman and said to Simon, "Do you see this woman? I entered your house; you gave Me no water for My feet, but she has washed My feet with her tears and wiped them with the hair of her head. You gave Me no kiss, but this woman has not ceased to kiss My feet since the time I came in. You did not anoint My head with oil, but this woman has anointed My feet with fragrant oil. Therefore I say to you, her sins, which are many, are forgiven, for she loved much. But to whom little is forgiven, the same loves little." Then He said to her, "Your sins are forgiven." Luke 7:45-48*

If only Jesus knew! Simon failed to understand that Jesus knew her inside and out: the good and the bad; her happiness and her sadness; her likes and dislikes. He knew everything about her, yet He welcomed her into His space. The heart of God is speaking concerning you. The same way the Pharisees tried to bring her past against her present and her possible future is the same way the enemy will try to condemn you. As I wrote in my book Diary of a girl, "You are not what you have done but you are what you have overcome." - Ritu Ghatourey. Not only Satan, but people will also try to throw the past in your face in efforts of keeping you down. Know that God wants to lavish you with unconditional love and forgiveness. Satan is calling you by your past, but the Lord is calling you by your future and who He has called you to be.

I feel as though some of you who are reading this are battling a war on the inside. A voice that keeps saying, "You are not good enough, everyone knows who you were, you think that you can just decide to change now? You will always be trash and nothing more."

God says, "You are forgiven, you are redeemed, and you are restored. My mercy covers you, My grace is around you and My love is unfailing, it has no end when it comes to you. I am the Lord who will always leave the ninety-nine in safety and run out to find you. Genuine repentance receives genuine forgiveness and I see the sincerity of your heart. I have called you forgiven, so accept the forgiveness I am giving you. Not only do I want you to accept my forgiveness but I also need you to forgive yourself. Your past means nothing to Me so stop trying to convince Me that you are not worthy enough; the dirtiest parts of your life could never make me love you any less. You are mine, you are loved, and you are forgiven."

"Your sins are forgiven; your faith has saved you, go in peace." *Luke 7: 48-50.* How delightful are the words that flow from the Master's mouth. In front of her tormentors she was forgiven and spoken to like a lady. God will put some people in their place concerning you, He is about to shut the mouth of the dragon and render men silent from

speaking ill of your name. Who God forgives and deems worthy, let no man dare condemn.

The Lord redeems the soul of His servants, and none of those who trust in Him shall be condemned. Psalm 34:22

Love keeps no record of wrong. Thus, whenever you feel condemnation from anyone, remember that forgiveness is always associated with love. If you question God's forgiveness towards you, you are questioning His unconditional love for you. Go in peace my sister; God's love and forgiveness are steadfast and unchanging. Walk in this so you can grow and glow in His glory.

Chapter 2

Resilience Through the Rejection

"**I** will give you Jacob for the night if you give me some of Reuben's mandrakes." Rachel's words were on repeat in my head. I was forced to walk in my sister's shadow from the time I was born. If that was not bad enough, my father made things worse when he tricked Jacob into marrying me knowing that he only wanted Rachel. The spotlight was never on me even if I was interested in having it. My sister's beauty captivated everyone and it caused her to have many under some kind of a spell of the sorts. Rejection has been a part of my life for a mighty long time, so I am accustomed to the feeling of abandonment. Be that as it may, it hurts like crazy that my husband is totally in love with the one person I could never compete with. They were many nights I sobbed inwardly without end from the pain. My heart desperately wants to be loved by Jacob, but will it ever happen? Maybe another son would do trick? If only he could look at me the way he looks at my sister. Sighhhhh." — *Leah*

Wikipedia's definition for resilience states: "The capacity to recover quickly from difficulties; toughness." I would like to introduce you to a woman named Leah who proved to be as resilient as a palm tree. She had the capability to recover from the constant misfortune she came up against. When the winds of the storm smashed into her, she would bend a little but she would never break. Her story depicts one so rich in resilience that I believe every Christian woman should possess such a spirit as hers. It is said that the greatest men and women alive are not super-people, but they are people who had great resilience.

From the beginning of her story in Genesis 29:17 we see her facing challenges. She is described as having delicate eyes; now we can ponder on what the author truly meant here and come up with our own conclusions. One thing for sure is that her delicate eyes would have had to be seen as a flaw in the eyes of man. When contrasting something to another thing, it usually means that they are different or total opposites. While the Bible describes Leah as having tender eyes, it goes on to say that her sister Rachel was beautiful of form and appearance. I can rightly assume that she was not as lovely to look at as her sister. Maybe she was the 'ugly duckling' by appearance in her family, but what she lacked in her outer beauty, she surely made up f or it in her inner beauty.

How hard would it have been to grow up with a beautiful sister who everyone adored and doted upon for her beauty, but when it came to you they would cringe? From her youth we see that Leah was dealt a bad hand of cards, but it never changed her tenderness, and I am not talking about her eyes. For me, she is one of the biblical wonder women I admire.

If you are familiar with the story, you are aware that Jacob fell in love with Rachel, but her father tricked him and he was given Leah on the night of the wedding. Was it that Laban thought Leah would never get married because of those tender eyes and thus he decided to secure her future deceitfully? She was given to a man who wanted her sister but got her in the package deal; this was truthfully a heart jerking situation. Leah ends up becoming the third wheel with a husband who did not want her and never loved her. How many of us would have a joyous attitude with this outcome?

When the sun shone bright the morning after their wedding night, Jacob more than likely had disgust written all over his face. What I admire most about Leah is that she didn't only possess the spirit of resilience, but she had a joy that never seemed to dim despite what she faced, and God saw that. He also saw that she was unloved and He opened her womb, but her sister Rachel was barren. Leah exclaimed, "The Lord has surely looked on my affliction," for she conceived a son whom she called him Reuben. What manner of woman is this who when faced with much rejection in the past and current state found it in herself to reverence the Lord? The answer to this is simple: a true woman of God. She could have chosen to take the same road as Peninnah in 1 Samuel Chapter one and be bitter or could have allowed her circumstances to destroy her, but she chose to keep bouncing back. She had a unique way of adjusting to the obstacles instead of allowing them to change her for the worse.

Leah gave birth to five more sons: Simeon, Levi, Judah, Issachar and Zebulun. With each child she held out hope that her husband would finally love her, but unfortunately he never did. This was a woman who had to 'hire' her husband from her sister in order to go to bed with him. As previously mentioned, she was a woman who lived in her sister's shadow from birth, a woman who probably had insecurity issues because of her tender eyes, a woman who was passed off as a pawn in her father's tricks, and a woman who craved love and affection from a man who had eyes for someone else. Even in spite of it all, Leah always did good by her husband. For she continued fearing the Lord, always having a positive attitude and never once turning bitter.

She was filled with an overcoming attitude and God used her to birth half of the tribe of Israel. She had the ability to hang on when it would have been easier to let go and turn her pain into hatred. At the end of her life, Leah was rewarded for her dedication to both her husband and her God. Eventually, she was buried next to Jacob but Rachel was not. Someone once said, "Many people are blessed with certain attributes, but resilience jumps to the forefront for success in any endeavour."

Maybe you have battled rejection all your life and it has paralyzed you. I want you adopt the spirit of resilience like Leah because it will give you the ability to recover and continue after your crisis. If you have read my first book Diary of Girl, you would know that I struggled with rejection issues for many years. I somehow liked the fact that God chose to share Leah's story with us because it helps me to see that things may not work out the way I want, but I still have to bounce back and move on with life. God revealed to me that regardless of who rejected me, I needed to be okay because He loved me. If the people we want to accept us never do, are we to turn bitter and let them ruin our lives? NO. Cope with the crisis and then successfully return to your pre-crisis state. That is what being resilient all is about.

Things will happen to us in life but how we let them

affect us, our attitude, our behaviour and our joy is totally up to us. Baby girl, learn how to reject rejection and move on. How about snapping back into shape today? I am not talking about physically but mentally and emotionally. Be like the palm tree and Leah, and learn how to snap back. You are resilient my dear, do not allow the spirit of rejection to break you.

Chapter 3

Going Through the Fire

"**I** am overwhelmed with such a deep sorrow and I must confess, it has left me bitter. Lorddd!! Why have you set your hand against me? My family was everything to me; yet you took them all away. If I am being honest, I do not want to face the reality of what has transpired. Maybe it's all a dream and I will wake up eventually. My world has spun out of control within a short space of time, and my heart isn't capable of handling it all. My darkest night is upon me; for that reason, I truly believe I will never see another bright star. What do I have left but a life I now do not want? *—Naomi*

The Heat – **The Fire**

The book of Ruth is usually spoken of from the standpoint of a spousal relationship, a story of a man who saved a woman and her mother-in-law. I want to dive into this text and give you a different revelation as it was given to me by God. We are going to have a look at the heat, the healer, the hurting, the helper and the hope. As women we go through a lot and we need to be there for each other. Naomi and Ruth's account gives us insight on how to help each other as sisters in Christ even while we are hurting.

Naomi experienced an out-of-control fire and I can only try to imagine how she felt. I did some research on the different types of burns online and they reminded me of the stages of Naomi's fire. There was a severe famine in Judah and her family moved to Moab in an effort to find sustainability. At some point Naomi's husband died from some unknown circumstance; we can refer to this as a second-degree burn. Second-degree burns involve the outer and middle layers of skin. The burn site appears red and blistered, and may be swollen and painful.

Most definitely, it would have been a painful situation for her to lose the man she loved and had been with for many years. It was devastating to say the least. After some time the Bible says that her sons Mahlon and Chilion got married. Perhaps she said to herself, "Okay, I lost my husband and it hurts insanely, but in the midst of it all I have gained two daughters and will soon have some grandkids." Despite the loss of the patriarch, the family was now multiplying. As great as that was, it did not last for too long because before she knew it, her sons had died as well.

This has now led her into her third degree burns. A third degree burn is also called a full thickness burn. Your skin contains three layers; therefore, the third degree burn occurs when all three layers are burned. Couldn't Naomi have gotten a break? What a tragic situation! Unfortunately, she had other things going against her in my opinion, which made her burns more severe. Back in Naomi's time, widows had no source of income; they depended heavily on their husbands or their sons. And so, how was she supposed to care for herself now that all her male relatives were gone?

We are now at the stage of the fifth degree burns. With a fifth degree burn, it penetrates the muscle and burns the bone. With these types of burns they receive less attention from doctors because they historically have a mortality rate of nearly 100 percent. These burns are so severe that they are usually only seen during an autopsy. It is almost impossible to survive this type of burn. When Naomi returned to her home town she was in such devastation that she called herself out of her name. What do I mean? She made everyone call her Mara (which means bitterness). *But she said to them, "Do not call me Naomi; call me Mara, for the Almighty has dealt very bitterly with me." Ruth 1:20.* She no longer considered herself Naomi; she was Mara, a woman who had lost everything. Bitterness, anger and hopelessness were her quota.

The Hurting – Naomi

It is quite obvious that Naomi was hurting, and hurting deeply. Physical fires hurt like hell, but know that emotional, mental and spiritual fires aren't any different when it comes to pain. If you are experiencing the heat right now here are a few points I would like you to take into consideration.

Ask God for Guidance

STOP, I repeat STOP telling everyone your business. Everyone is not entitled to a front row seat of your life. This does not mean that you are to hide up and suffer in silence. It means that you need to go to God and find out who to talk to and also when to talk. Every listening ear isn't a help, some people are simply looking for the next gossip. Be open but know who to open up to. The Lord is the best advisor when it comes to these things. Say "God, who do you want me to speak to concerning this trial I am currently experiencing?"

Learn How to Encourage Yourself

Truth be told, you can hear all the inspiration in the world but when you go home at night and no one is around, you still have your situation to deal with. Encouragement from others is good, but nothing really ever beats self-encouragement. Occasionally you have to beat self-pity with a stick over its head and remember who you are and whose you are and what God can do for you. You have to look in the mirror and say "I got this, I believe in you, I am an overcomer, I am not a quitter, victory is mine." You may not always feel like doing it, but do it anyway. Without self-motivation we can sometimes slip into depression quickly, but when we encourage ourselves in the Lord, we remove the focus from our issue and we begin to remember that God is our strength.

Eventually Use Your Pain as Power

I am of the belief that our pain should always be turned into power and purpose. Someone out there will benefit from the journey of your fire. It may not seem like it right now but your story will be a catalyst for someone else's healing. The same way we encourage ourselves is the same way we need to get over ourselves as well and know that it isn't always about us. At some point we will need to stop the whining, stop taking the baby bottle and turn that pain into purpose. Look at how I used the pain of my past to write my first book and here I am now on my fourth. I am not saying that you have to do a 'tell all book,' but I am certain God has a plan of action for your present discomfort. Ask Him for insight and revelation on how to use your story for your growth and for His glory.

The Healer – God

Jehovah Rapha, the God who heals spiritually, physically,

emotionally and mentally. *"For I am the Lord who heals you."* *Exodus 15:26 NLT.* Unknown to Naomi and Ruth, God had a plan for the both of them and that plan included healing from their brokenness. She was quick to say that she went out full, and the Lord had brought her home empty. *"Why do you call me Naomi, since the Lord has testified against me, and the Almighty has afflicted me?"* *Ruth 1:21.*

Looking at things from a natural stand point, Naomi believed that she had come back to Judah empty. She left Judah with her husband and two sons and here she was returning with a daughter-in-law only. *So Naomi returned, and Ruth the Moabitess her daughter-in-law with her, who returned from the country of Moab. Now they came to Bethlehem at the beginning of barley harvest. Ruth 1:22.* Naomi may have felt like she came back in empty but she came back home right on time, at the beginning of the barley harvest. It signified the harvest of their healing, the harvest of their redemption, the harvest of their restoration and the harvest of their joy. The Healer was in the midst of the fire even though she felt as if His hand was against her.

Could Naomi be healed from her fifth degree burns? She sure could and she definitely was healed. The doctors see it physically impossible for a human to survive from such burns. The enemy is trying to make you believe that healing is unattainable after fifth degree burns, but I am here to tell you that he is a big fat liar. Jehovah Rapha, the healer Himself wants to bring healing to your charred bones.

The Helper – Ruth

We all know that Holy Spirit is the number one Helper; nevertheless, the helper I am referring to here is Ruth. From hindsight we can see and presume that Naomi's fire was more intense than Ruth's. We will all face challenges in life, but there will be times when our condition won't be as severe as the other person. Who in your life is facing daunting circumstances? Are they on the brink of giving up? Remind them of God's faithfulness and His promises. Perhaps today you are the one helping another sister battle her fire, here is some advice I would like to leave with you.

Make Sure You are Hearing From God

It is my belief that Ruth heard from God and that was the reason she stayed with Naomi when she had all reasons to leave. Nothing good in Judah was waiting for her, this was a place where Moabites were considered harlots. She knew very well that if she went on with Naomi to Judah, chances are she won't ever marry again. How would both of them as women survive without male provision? She would have a better life if she stayed in Moab, but despite all the odds stacked against her she still went ahead to Judah. Perhaps she called it a gut feeling or something else, but I believe God quickened her spirit and gave her a peace about going with Naomi. Flesh and blood did not reveal that to her, she received some form of revelation from God.

If you want to be a help someone who is hurting from a fire, you need to be tuned into the voice of God. Helping without God is harmful. It is imperative for you to lean on God to help others because even though they may be experiencing a similar situation you've been through before, it will not be the same. Seek the face of the Lord to hear what He wants you to say or do for the person you are helping or intend to help.

Be Trustworthy

Ruth did not go around Judah divulging Naomi's business to everyone. How can someone confide in you if you are not trustworthy? Many people go through fires alone because they are afraid of their personal issues becoming the next topic of gossip around the church. If you know you have a problem with keeping your mouth closed then you NEED to ask God for help in this matter.

Be Selfless

Just because you yourself are hurting, it does not mean you cannot help someone else. Bear in mind that Ruth was also nursing wounds from the pain of losing her husband, yet she looked past her pain and made sure she was there for Naomi. In spite of reading the book of Ruth countless times, it never dawned on me the level of selflessness she displayed.

She did not run off helping Naomi in the hopes of gaining anything. Her main focus was providing and caring for her mother-in-law, which led her into the fields to be a reaper. Hence, because of her selfless nature she was rewarded by God. Do you know that in your hurt you can still help? If you want God to use you then you need to adopt the spirit of selflessness. It makes no sense saying "God here I am, use me", then when He sends you to someone you throw a big pity party bash. "God not right now, check back with me in a couple months, I am dealing with my own issues." The Lord is looking for a set of people who will go out amidst the hurt because they know that it's all about Him and not them. It is beautiful to me how most of the time when we put our problems aside and help others, our issue then works itself out.

Be Humble

You cannot help if you believe you never need any help. I have a serious problem with people who believe they never need help but are always ready to help others. Is it a case of pride? I would leave it up to you to call it whatever seems fit; nonetheless, we must not walk around believing we are above help.

The Hope – God

Now may the God of hope fill you with all joy and peace in believing, that you may abound in hope by the power of the Holy Spirit. Romans 15:13

When we are experiencing a trial by fire it is a blessing to have people around who are positive and motivating. Naomi had given up all hope; she was in a sullen state from all of her acquired burns. "God has dealt bitterly with me," she said. Ruth was a positive influence during her mother-in-law's predicament, though she, too, was carrying her own pain. I am sure that Ruth reminded Naomi of the God she had introduced her to when she came into the family.

Have you lost your hope as Naomi did? Let me reintroduce you to the Hope, God. Going through the heat without hope is gruelling. Leah went through a heat but she had a hope, thus her attitude was pleasant and joyful. Naomi went through the heat without a hope and it left her nasty and bitter. If you're not currently facing a fire, know that you will in the future. Leah and Naomi adopted two different responses because of the fires they encountered; may I ask which one of these ladies would you rather be? Would it be the one who had joy in spite of it all, or the one who was quite grumpy all the way through?

Have you ever heard the term trial by fire? It is the test of one's ability to perform well under pressure. So how are

32

you performing under pressure? All was well in the end of this story. Ruth married Boaz who perpetuated the name of her late husband through his inheritance and his name was not cut off. Naomi was now beaming with happiness; something good was finally happening after all the grief.

You are sleeping peacefully but the smell of smoke alarms you to the fire that has started unknown to you while you were resting. Your first plan of action is to run outside to get away from the clouds of smoke, but upon touching the knob of the bedroom door, your hand is scorched immensely from the heat. "Water!!!" You whisper. You scurry to the master bedroom in hopes of turning on the shower to cool down the room until you hatch a plan of escape. Hiding away in the bathtub, you perceive that the water isn't doing much because the inhalation of smoke, gases, and vapours seeping through the bedroom are beginning to strangle you. There are terrifying sounds of the wood splitting along a crevice and releasing steam into the fire, the screams of the people outside are becoming faint as your lungs become blocked from the toxins, rendering you into a semi unconscious state. You indistinctly hear a voice saying "It's okay, I got you." You are pulled from the wreckage and an oxygen mask is placed on your face as you are being rushed to the paramedics in hopes that you will make it. "I feel a

pulse!" one person shouted. "She is going to be fine," another chummed in. "She came out of that and lived? She is blessed," another ended. Newspaper article the next day reads: "HOW DID SHE EVEN SURVIVE?"

You have caused men to ride over our heads; we went through fire and through water; But You brought us out to rich fulfilment. Psalm 66:12. Sis, be strengthened in heart and in body; God will bring you through the fire. He doesn't always save us from our trials, but He does save us in our trials. No matter what He allows you to go through, and no matter how heavy the weight may be, He will be with you.

Chapter 4

It Is Well

"Τhis is definitely the worst day of my life; nothing could have prepared me for what I'm currently going through. My child is lying motionless on Elisha's bed where I rested him. I'm feeling dizzy; my head is throbbing; my heart hurts as if there's an open wound which is being repeatedly punctured. And my limbs, they too are numb; yet I'm journeying relentlessly towards the man of God in search of a miracle. The same God who gave me this beautiful boy can surely bring him back to life again. Memories of him keep flashing before my face as the tears cascade upon my cheeks. Yet, somehow, in the midst of everything, my heart keeps singing a tune, 'It is well'." **– The Shunammite Woman**

When peace, like a river, attendeth my way, When sorrows like sea billows roll; whatever my lot, Thou hast taught me to say, It is well, it is well with my soul. – Horatio G. Spafford

Horatio G. Spafford was a prominent lawyer who lived in Chicago with his wife and five children. Their young son died in 1871 from pneumonia, and in that same year, their business was lost in a fire. Hard, right? It gets even crazier. In 1873, Mrs. Spafford and their four daughters took sail to Europe where Mr. Spafford was supposed to join them a few days later. Unfortunately, their plans came to a shattering end because the ship that they were on collided with another ship and sank. The four Spafford children died, but his wife survived by floating on a piece of the wreckage. She wired her husband a message, which began, "Saved alone, what shall I do?" Hurriedly, Mr. Spafford made a booking on the next available ship to join his grieving wife. As he sailed across the sea to meet her, he wrote the song titled, "It Is Well With My Soul."

How could this man lose so much, yet still have the strength to put pen to paper and say *"It is well with my soul."* Can we truthfully be well in adversity? Can we be well when mourning the loss of loved ones, when there are major financial challenges, health issues, broken marriages or when our lives just fall apart for whatever reason? Yes, we can; however, the key to being well while suffering is 'God'.

The Shunammite's woman story in 2 Kings Chapter 4:8 -37 is the perfect example to inspect if we want to talk about being well when our world, as we see it, falls apart. Her story begins when she decided to be hospitable to Elisha the prophet by giving him a room above her home for whenever he travelled through Shunem. Her kindness did not go unnoticed, and Elisha wanted to show appreciation by being a blessing to her for being cordial and generous towards him and his servant. After offering to speak to the king on her behalf, and hearing her quick refusal, he questioned his servant Gehazi on what could be done for the notable woman.

"Yessss I got it!" belted Gehazi to Elisha.

It dawned on him what could be done for the Shunammite woman. She was childless, and her husband was quite old in age, surely she would love to have a child of her own.

"About this time next year you shall embrace a son of your own." These words gently rolled from Elisha's tongue and left her in shock.

She bawled, "No, my Lord! Man of God, do not lie to your maidservant."

Here it was that Elisha brought her inner secret desire to surface. What she yearned for was now known. She may have been longing for a child for many years and becoming hopeless with each passing year, but now he was telling her that she would conceive and give birth to a son.

As Elisha would have prophesied, it came to pass when the appointed time was at hand that she conceived and gave birth to a son. What a glorious story so far, right? Now here is where it all went downhill rather quickly. Years had passed and the child grew. One day while in the field, he informed his father that he was feeling unwell, and he was carried to his mother. She held him on her knees as a mother usually does, trying to nurture and reassure her sick child that everything was going to be alright, but unfortunately, he passed away.

She took him up to the man of God's room, laid him on the bed, shut the door behind her, and went on her way. She then called to her husband and said, "Please send me one of the young men and one of the donkeys that I may run to the man of God and come back." He replied, "Why are you going to him today? It is neither the New Moon nor the Sabbath." And she said, "It is well." 2 King 4:22-23.

Now let's have a real conversation here. I don't know about you, but for me, this woman seemed exceptionally calm to be in such a position as this. The child she gave birth to, whom she cherished and loved dearly, had just died in her arms and she was telling her husband that all was well. But was it well? Was she in denial? Their son was lying cold and lifeless not far from where they stood and she was calmer than a baby taking its bottle. I, however, admire that her first instinct was not to panic, it was not to scream nor was it to 'lose her mind'; her first thought was to set out in search of the man of God.

This woman had faith that God could make her situation better. Unlike some of us who go to the phone before we visit the throne, she sought out the prophet of God first. You do realise that she did not tell her husband the problem, right? She ran to the Man of God because she discerned that he knew the Lord intimately. God was the only one she felt could bring light to her dark situation.

Just as the Shunammite woman and Mr. Spafford sought God in their crisis, we need to do the same as well. Sometimes when we run off exposing our 'business' to people, it only makes the matter worse. Some folks would encourage you to give up hope about the dead things in your life, merely because they breathe negativity and disbelief, and that is something you should avoid at all cost. Can I dare to tell you that only God knows if the dry bones can live? Let us continue with her story and see if she continues to be well. After speaking to her husband, she saddled the donkey and went out on her way to look for the man of God. Elisha saw her from afar and sent Gehazi to meet her to make sure everything was okay, but once again she said, "It is well."

When she came to the man of God at the hill, she

caught him by the feet, but Gehazi came near to push her away. But the man of God said, "Let her alone; for her soul is in deep distress, and the Lord has hidden it from me, and has not told me." So she said, "Did I ask a son of my lord? Did I not say, 'Do not deceive me'?" Then he said to Gehazi, "Get yourself ready, and take my staff in your hand, and be on your way. If you meet anyone, do not greet him; and if anyone greets you, do not answer him; but lay my staff on the face of the child." And the mother of the child said, "As the Lord lives, and as your soul lives, I will not leave you." So he arose and followed her. 2 Kings 4: 27-30

When the Shunammite woman reached Elisha, she fell down at his feet and all the pain she was experiencing flowed out. Was she a hypocrite for saying all was well and now she was weeping at his feet? NO. Just because she said it was well that did not mean that she was exempt from the hurt of seeing her son lifeless. Take note of what Spafford said, "When in peace and when in sorrow I will still say it is well."

The Lord had given her her heart's desire and now it was being stripped away. I consider her to be a woman of strong faith. The same God who had given her the son she always dreamt about, was able to restore life into his dead body. In this world as Christians, we will have tribulations. We do not get excused from the hardships of this fallen world, but how we handle the hardships will say a lot about our faith in God. As Job exclaimed, "though he slay me yet will I trust in Him."

When Elisha came into the house, there was the child, lying dead on his bed. He went in therefore, shut the door behind the two of them, and prayed to the Lord. And he went up and lay on the child, and put his mouth on his mouth, his eyes on his eyes, and his hands on his hands; and he stretched himself out on the child, and the flesh of the child became warm. He returned and walked back and forth in the house, and again went up and stretched himself out on him; then the child sneezed seven times, and the child opened his eyes. And he called Gehazi and said, "Call this Shunammite woman." So he called her. And when she came in to him, he said, "Pick up your son." So she went in, fell at his feet, and bowed to the ground; then she picked up her son and went out. 2 Kings 4:32-37

Death was defied and her son was revived to life. What if this was your story? What would have been your response? How many of us can lose so much like Mr. Spafford and this woman, and still confidently say it is well? When faced with terrifying and life altering obstacles, how will you react? God wants to help you grow in such a way that your faith is strong in Him, that hulk Hogan type of strong that when trials knock at your door no matter what they may be, you will say "It is well with my soul."

"Be still oh worried heart, know that I am God and I will comfort you in the Chaos." – God

A deep relationship with your God will bring such an attitude. Know that as His daughter, He has your back, more than any earthly father ever could. Are you willing to say "Lord, teach me how to be well even when my world falls completely apart"? Ask the Lord to give you a heart that will rest in His loving embrace, even when the seas of life roar and the thunder of your emotions shatters you. Whatever your lot and whatever your portion, it can be well with you, as long as your faith and your confidence in God is unwavering.

It Is Well

Everything never goes according to my will,
I never understand why my situations are so ill.
There is much stress,
But I always give of my best
My drive just wont allow me to rest.

I am confident in Him,
Although things may appear grim.
God always comes through for me,
At times I may never see.
He mends my broken pieces making me whole;
It is always well with my soul.
— Khadija Collymore

Chapter 5

God's Miracle – My Faith

"**S**hame, sadness, helplessness and anxiety is how I am feeling at this point. How do I cope with not only losing a husband but also the possibility of losing my sons? I know for certain that I won't survive emotionally if they are taken away from me. My husband was a good man, one who feared and served the Lord faithfully, so why was this all happening to me? Maybe, just maybe the man of God Elisha could help me figure out what I should do. I have seen and heard about the miraculous things that have happened through him. Perhaps he can petition God on my behalf." – *The Widow*

> A certain woman of the wives of the sons of the prophets cried out to Elisha, saying, "Your servant my husband is dead, and you know that your servant feared the LORD. And the creditor is coming to take my two sons to be his slaves." So Elisha said to her, "What shall I do for you? Tell me, what do you have

in the house?" And she said, "Your maidservant has nothing in the house but a jar of oil." Then he said, "Go, borrow vessels from everywhere, from all your neighbors—empty vessels; do not gather just a few. And when you have come in, you shall shut the door behind you and your sons; then pour it into all those vessels, and set aside the full ones." So she went from him and shut the door behind her and her sons, who brought the vessels to her; and she poured it out. Now it came to pass, when the vessels were full, that she said to her son, "Bring me another vessel." And he said to her, "There is not another vessel." So the oil ceased. Then she came and told the man of God. And he said, "Go, sell the oil and pay your debt; and you and your sons live on the rest." 2 Kings 4:1-7

A widow, her sons, the debt, a jar of oil and a big God are all ingredients for the baking of a miraculous story. Pull up a chair, get comfy, and turn your Bible to 2 Kings Chapter 4 in order for us to follow the account of the widow who was placed in an unfortunate situation and came out on top. I can use many words to describe her circumstance: destitute, desolate, traumatizing, desperate and stressful. My intention is to make it extremely clear for you the volume of pressure she was under. Her husband had died, she was left in debt, and the creditors were intending to take her sons away. In those days, the person who owed the debt, along with his family, could have been sold as a form of payment. You can draw reference from the story of the unforgiving servant in Matthew Chapter 18 to fully understand what I mean. The man and his entire family were about to be sold because he was unable to pay his debt.

This widow was grieving the loss of her husband, worrying about her finances, stressing about the creditors taking her sons and wondering how she was going to survive day by day without any source of income or work skills. Just as some may brand her situation as hopeless, I sense the Holy Spirit telling me that you are in a predicament which you have labelled 'hopeless'; the weight of everything happening all at once is too heavy to bear and the anxiety is beginning to take you under. My beautiful sister, this woman's story does not end here and neither does yours. Stay with me on this journey and see how God brought her out.

Just like the Shunammite woman, the first thing she did when she realized she needed help was to cry out to the man of God for a word from the Lord. Where does your help come from? Who do you first run to when facing a trial? See what Psalm 34:17 states: *The righteous cry out, and the LORD hears, and delivers them out of all their troubles.* Often times when troubles arise in our lives, the first action we take is to either message or call our friends for guidance, support, encouragement and help. It's all good to want the comfort of a friend when at a low state in your life, but you need to grasp the fact that God is your ultimate source, the only One who truly knows your situation and can make the impossible become possible. He is the One you first need to cry out to before you take your problems elsewhere; the solution to your problem is found in the Problem Solver.

When the Israelites were being oppressed in Egypt, they cried out and the Lord heard their groaning. His heart was moved with compassion and He sent them a deliverer. When blind Bartimaeus cried out to Jesus even though the people wanted him to be quiet, Jesus came to his side and healed him. When David cried out to God many times, God came into his situation and rescued him. Do you see the trend here? When we cry out to the Lord, He hears us and does not forsake us; moreover, He delivers us from our trouble. Crying out displays humility and surrender because it shows that you cannot solve what you are going through on your own. You are therefore acknowledging God's ability to provide. It's not in your own strength but by His Spirit.

After pouring your heart out to God for a breakthrough, remember to take the time to listen to Him for instructions. We talk way too much when we go before the Lord, not comprehending that we also have to listen to what He wants to say. Have you ever had a one-sided conversation with someone? They talk, and talk, and talk, and you never get the chance to get a word in? It is highly annoying and rude. It's time you stop doing that with God. When you cry out, be prepared to wait and listen to hear what He has to say.

In verse 2, Elisha asked the widow about what she had in her house. She replied, "Your maidservant has nothing in the house but a jar of oil." Dear queen, you have something on the inside of you that is connected to the solution for your problem. The widow figured that she had nothing to offer, but her nothing, when placed in the hands of God, would multiply and become something. Moses' rod was used to part the Red Sea; a jawbone of a donkey was used by Samson to kill one thousand men; and a little boy's fish and bread were used to feed thousands of people. When their nothings were placed in the Lord's hand, it was used to produce a miracle, and this widow's story isn't any different. The next time God asks you what you have, let this be the response: "I only have a (insert thing) Lord; notwithstanding, I know when given to You it is more than enough. You are the God of multiplication and I ask that you turn my nothing into something for Your honour."

Moving along, we see Elisha laying out a plan for the widow. He told her to go and borrow the vessels from her neighbours. This is where her obedience and work of faith comes in. We say time and time again that obedience is better than sacrifice and faith without works is dead, but do we really believe what we say? Picture being low in spirit, feeling ashamed that you are in debt and the Lord is sending you to borrow from your neighbours.

Her friends probably thought that since she lost her husband, she was now losing her mind. I can envision the stares and gossip that surrounded her and how she had to set self and pride aside to achieve what was required of her to do. I honestly believe that this action was a test of faith; and she passed with flying colours. She stepped out in faith and walked in obedience when she got the word. It makes no sense for you to ask God to give you a breakthrough and when He asks you to do something you refuse. If one thing is clear from reading the Word, when obedience is exercised, a miracle is not far behind. You have a part to play as well.

Elisha then instructed the widow to shut the door behind her and her sons and fill all of the empty jars until none were remaining. Why did Elisha tell her to shut the door? When Peter went to revive Dorcas to life, he shut the door behind the weeping widows. When Jesus went to do the same for the little girl, He shut the door behind the doubtful people who were saying she was already dead and He was too late. When Elisha raised the Shunammite's son, he went in and shut the door behind her and his servant.

Sometimes you have to shut the door on the negativity, doubt and fear that people will try to bring. As humans, people read the outcome of situations by physical sight; they analyse your situation based on facts. They say "How will you get that bill paid when you have no money?" The problem is that they lack faith; the fact is that you have no money, but the truth is that you are seeing through your eyes of faith, knowing that God will come through. When you relay to them what you are hoping, they may begin to sow seeds of doubt because of their unbelief. So, when God tells you to do something 'run hard' and fast to shut the door upon any and all negative energy.

Upon following all of Elisha's instructions, the jars were all filled, and then the widow returned to him to find out what to do. Notice, she did not come up with a plan of her own. What I have realized over the years of this faith walk is that God doesn't always give us a play by play initially, sometimes He leaves out parts of the plan so that we don't get besides ourselves and forget that He is our source. When the Lord gives you something to do, always go back to Him to find out what your next step is.

We are reaching the glorious end of the story, but it's really the beginning of a new life for this widow and her sons. In verse 7, Elisha tells her to sell the jars of oil, pay her debt, and live on the rest of the money. God not only provided a solution to the problem, He also gave her more than enough and she was swimming in His abundance. The money gained would have been plentiful, because she was able to pay her debt and live on the rest.

You have been asking God for a miracle, but my question to you is, are you ready? Are you ready to follow instructions when God tells you the plan? Are you ready to put works to your faith? Are you ready to shut out the people who are hindering your miracle? Are you ready to put the time aside for God so you can commune with Him?

You want to walk in the abundance of the miracle but are you ready to do the work, sis? Your miracle is in the room if you will only grab hold of it. God wants to do something extraordinary in your life, but you will need to position yourself. Faith plays an important role in your spiritual growth; so my question to you is: Is your faith increasing or is it still the mustard seed size? The Lord wants you to have unshakable faith.

Oceans

My enemies like grains of sand
So few beneath my feet
But a multitude surrounding me.
You beckon me into the water
And I run, slip and slide,
In an effort to reach you
But as the waves caress my toes
And my enemies are pulled from under me
I realise....
I can't swim.

You look at me expectantly,
Hands outstretched
As you stand on the water
It almost seems effortless.
Even though the waves crash violently
Against the shores,
It is nothing compared to the storm within me.
I am tempted to turn back,
Take my chances with the devil,
But instead I go one step further.

I plead for you to help me
With desperation in my eyes
You keep your arms outstretched
And simply smile.
But Jesus I don't understand.
I have faith that you will
Part the sea and let me walk through.
You laugh and shake your head

53

A Girl and Her GOD

Saying that I must come to you.
So I take a deep breath.

Inhaling the salt and waves,
I run into the water
Screaming nothing but your name.
The wind is knocked out of me
And replaced with water
Rushing into my lungs.
But instead of feeling suffocated
I feel cleansed.
The next breath I take is entirely by faith
And to my surprise it is oxygen.

I open my eyes to see yours.
Flames of judgement yet
as comforting as the hearth at Christmas.
Your smile full of love
And your voice full of tenderness,
You gather me in an embrace
And say, "It's about time."
I look down and we're both standing on water.
Sometimes I need you to remind me that
drowning in you, is walking on water.
© Janielle Browne

Chapter 6

Grace In the Wilderness

"**I**s this the end? Is it even possible for a person's soul to physically ache? Well, that's how I feel. The dryness of my mouth reminds me of my current situation as I'm about to slip into another hallucination. I am very exhausted because of the heat and lack of water. Sadly, I must confess that my strength is failing as I sit helplessly listening to my son cry out in anguish from his thirst. This was not the plan. They told me that if I gave birth to a son everything would be fine. They even said that I would be well cared for, but it was all a lie. The piercing sound of Ishmael's loud screams brought me back to the matter at hand; we are in a wasteland with no possibility of sustenance. I remember the prophecy from the God who heard me when I was pregnant many years ago. Surely the Lord who visited me previously in that wilderness can probably visit me now. I have exhausted all measures and this is my only hope. So I weep and shout out with all the strength left within me in hopes of one more encounter with the God who sees." – *Hagar*

In the midst of a wilderness experience of life we can find comfort in the grace of God. What happens when God does not bring us out of the wilderness but rather clothes us fully in grace while in the wilderness? Let us see.

Thus says the Lord, "The people who survived the sword found grace in the wilderness – Israel, when I went to give him rest." Jeremiah 31: 2

There is a woman in the Bible who survived the sword and found exceptional grace in God in the wilderness, her name is Hagar. I have come to the conclusion over the years of being a Christian that many people often paint a bad picture of her. More often than not, she is always viewed as the disgruntled outside woman. However, I see her in a different light and in my opinion; she was an exceptionally strong woman.

Let us go back to the beginning of her story before we get to her wilderness experience. God had spoken to Abraham about the promised heir from his loins, but after not seeing it come to pass, Sarah grew impatient and decided to take matters into her own hands. She thought it best to give her maidservant Hagar, the Egyptian, to Abraham, in order to obtain a child. In Sarah's mind, she was old and unable to conceive, therefore, her best bet was to get Hagar to do the job and give them the heir God had spoken about. I want to stop right here for a minute.

Take a look at Hagar's plight; envision not having any say whatsoever in your life as a slave. To make matters worse, you are now given to your master's husband and any objections cannot be voiced. The child you did not ask to carry will not be considered your son, but Sarah's own.

The Bible says that Sarah became despised in Hagar's sight. Many people have automatically come to the assumption that Hagar had become spiteful because she was now pregnant by Abraham; something Sarah was unable to do. But was she moving out of spitefulness? Couldn't it be that she despised Sarah because of the situation she had placed her in? Whatever the reason, Hagar was dealt so harshly by her mistress that she fled from her presence into the wilderness.

In Genesis 16: 7-9, the angel of the Lord found her by a spring of water in the wilderness and encouraged her to return to her mistress. She was informed of her pregnancy and he told her the name to give her son, and a word of prophecy was also given to her about Ishmael's future. She was content with her visit from God, amused at the fact that the Lord visited her, a mere Egyptian slave. She returned to her unfortunate circumstance under the submission of Sarah.

A Girl and Her GOD

Everything seemed to be 'okay' until chapter 21 when Isaac is born. The promised son was now in the picture, which meant that Ishmael was cast further aside. Being that Sarah detested Hagar, I am confident she had some kind of distaste towards Ishmael as well. One day Sarah caught Ishmael scoffing at her son and told Abraham to send him away. In her words, "Ishmael could never be heir with Isaac." I want you to think for a minute and look deeper into this situation.

Could it be that Ishmael scoffed at his brother because he felt rejected? Having read and pondered on the story, it seems quite clear to me that Ishmael would have been treated as a second option. He probably felt as if he was never good enough for his father, unlike his brother, the promised son, who was. When I read the account in this light, my heart started to bleed for both mother and child. They had to endure a hapless life they never asked for. How would one feel as a mother to see her son being rejected by the very two people who wanted her to have him? Hagar and her son were more than likely broken-hearted.

When Sarah asked Abraham to send his son away, he was somewhat displeased. Nevertheless, God instructed him to do what Sarah had asked. Did God send Hagar in the wilderness? Yes, He surely did. The Lord allowed Abraham to send them away; it was not that they were horrible people.

The fact is, Isaac was always the one destined to fulfil the promise; Ishmael came about because of the impatience of man. The two brothers could never grow and dwell in the same place. What I need you to understand is that even though God chose Isaac, he never once rejected Ishmael or his mother. Let that sink in.

Abraham sent them away with bread and a skin of water which would have been enough to ensure their survival. They departed and wandered into the wilderness of Beersheba. Hagar once again was faced with another wilderness experience. God had brought her out of the first one, would He do it again? When all of the water in the skin was gone, Hagar placed her son under a shrub and sat at a distance from him. She wanted to be close to him, but still did not want to see him die of thirst and hunger. She definitely believed that it was the end for them; there was no more water and death was ringing at their door. There was nowhere to go and no one to turn too; hope had finally 'departed.'

Are you facing your wilderness and presume that it is the end? Think again, hope again, and believe again; watch how it all worked out for Hagar and be assured that it can happen for you as well. In her despair, Hagar did not perceive that the same God who allowed her to be sent into the wilderness would give her the grace to live in it. The same God who brought her out before would find a way to bring peace to her life.

When she lifted up her voice and cried out for her son and their situation, the angel of the Lord said, "What ails you Hagar, fear not." Pause here again for a moment and just give a loud praise unto the Lord of hosts. Upon reading this for the hundredth time and now seeing these words with fresh revelation, God spoke deeply to me about my current situation and told me to speak to you.

God is saying "What ails you (insert your name)? Fear not, for I am with you and I have a plan for your life. This wilderness will not be the death of you. I own the cattle on a thousand hills, I stopped the sun from going down for Joshua, I opened the eyes of the blind, what is your problem to Me?"

Now let's get back to the word and see how the Lord graced Hagar. He opened her eyes, and she was able to see a well of water to sustain her and the boy. Listen to me, my sister, God wants to open your eyes spiritually and show you that you will be sustained in the midst of wilderness.

So God was with the lad; and he grew and dwelt in the wilderness, and became an archer. He dwelt in the Wilderness of Paran; and his mother took a wife for him from the land of Egypt. Genesis 21: 20-21

Did you just read what I read? Hagar did not leave the

wilderness. This was not a Red Sea moment or a Jericho moment where God delivered them from their issue the same time. Hagar and her son dwelt in the wilderness, an uncultivated and uninhabited place where they were blessed. How can you be blessed in the wasteland of life? It is the grace of God, my darling.

I cannot promise you that God will bring you out of your wilderness right now. What I can and will tell you is that His grace will cover you no matter where you are. Many of us fail to understand this type of grace and so we miss it. It is a grace of not knowing how it will come together in the end, but as of now, you just ride the waves. It is a grace that says "I am living pay check to pay check because my money isn't enough, but every single month food is on the table and my bills are paid." Do you understand the grace that I am referring to? Hagar and Ishmael grew, ate, slept, laughed, built and Ishmael even married in the wilderness. Are you grasping what I am trying to tell you? Some of you are looking for God to take you out of your wilderness, but what if He wants to keep you there for a longer period of time?

As I am writing this chapter, God is quickening my spirit to the fact that this is what He is currently doing with me. I have been experiencing my own desert for years now with no end in sight. The Lord just told me that I have been trying to escape from a place that I need to reside in a while longer. Hear this, when you are on a mountain living gloriously and flourishing, it's lovely. But know that when you are in the darkest of valleys, and God always finds ways to keep blessing you and putting you on top; it brings glory to His name. More often than not, when people see that you are being blessed in a drought, it makes them ask how you accomplishing such. And with great pleasure, you point them to God.

How are you making it each day, each month and each hour when the stacks are against you at every turn? It is nothing but the grace of the Lord. I would rather be in the wilderness clothed with the grace of God than be anywhere else without His grace. God wants you to grow and glow in Him even in your wilderness period. His grace abounds in the deepest of waters and the driest of deserts.

And God is able to make all grace abound toward you, that you, always having all sufficiency in all things, may have an abundance for every good work. 2 Corinthians 9:8

Your Grace Is sufficient

Even in the wilderness about to take my last breath,
I'll trust you Lord with all of me
And know you will supply my needs.
You are my rock and you are my shield,
This is why I'll always kneel.
In distress or raging seas,
I know you will take care of me...

The enemy has tried his best
To make my life into a mess.
Despite it all I will press on
And show God's power in my storm.
Your grace is what is keeping me
The enemy will have to flee.
I'll lift my hands I'll lift my voice,
And praise the God who sees it all.
— Shaniqua L. Howell

Chapter 7

A Woman Who Fears the Lord

"There is no way I am doing what he has asked. I want no part of his plan to destroy these innocent babies. Cruel is not a proper word to describe him, it is as if he has gone mad. We stand a chance of being punished if found being disobedient, but I can live with that, can you? What I cannot live with, is the distaste from the Lord for taking part in such wickedness. My hands shall be clean of this and I shall follow the marching orders from God to do what is right. Are you with me, Puah? – *Shiphrah*

Then the king of Egypt spoke to the Hebrew midwives, of whom the name of one was Shiphrah and the name of the other Puah; and he said, "When you do the duties of a midwife for the Hebrew women, and see them on the birthstools, if it is a son, then you shall kill him; but if it is a daughter, then she shall live." But the midwives feared God, and did not do as the king of Egypt commanded them, but saved the male children alive. So the king of Egypt called for the midwives and said to them, "Why have you done this thing, and saved the male children alive?" And the midwives said to Pharaoh, "Because the Hebrew women are not like the Egyptian women; for they are lively and give birth before the midwives come to them." Therefore God dealt well with the midwives, and the people multiplied and grew very mighty. And so it was, because the midwives feared God, that He provided households for them. Exodus 1:15-21

The Bible speaks on two types of fear. The first type of fear is the fear of the Lord. It does not mean that we should be necessarily afraid of Him; rather, it is a reverential awe of Him. The fear of the Lord brings with it many blessings and benefits. It is the beginning of wisdom and leads to good understanding (Psalm 111:10); it provides security (Proverbs 14:26); it adds length to life (Proverbs 10:27); and it also enables a person to avoid evil (Proverbs 3:7).

The second type of fear mentioned in the Bible is not a benefit to the believer but a destiny killer; this is the "spirit of fear" mentioned in 2 Timothy 1:7. It states: "For God has not given us a spirit of fear, but of power and of love and of a sound mind." Throughout the Bible, God encourages us to "Fear not." The fear of the Lord is to be promoted, and the spirit of fear is to be overcome.

Shiphrah and Puah were women who feared the Lord

and did not entertain the spirit of fear. These women are not spoken about much today, but their bravery is exceptional to me. Their reverence for God was greater than Pharaoh and his command.

The people of Israel were multiplying rapidly and Pharaoh was afraid of them taking over. Resultantly, he hatched a plan to deal with them harshly in an effort that they stop increasing in number; however, the more He afflicted them, the more they multiplied and grew exceedingly. In his next attempt to control the vast number of people of Israel, he went to the midwives Shiphrah and Puah, and commanded them to kill all the male children born at their hands. The easiest solution would have been to listen to the king and do as he advised, but they didn't.

Who actually refuses a king? Their actions would have been punishable by death if found guilty. One might say that they were placed in a tough situation, but for them there was only one option, and it was not in Pharaoh's favour.

The Bible tells us that the midwives feared God, and hence, they defied the very decree the king had made. If placed in the same position, what do you think your response would have been in the matter? Furthermore, when you find yourself in a similar situation to this what will you do? Will your fear of the Lord be greater than man, or will you succumb to doing wrong because of the spirit of fear?

Standing up and doing what is right isn't always easy, but it is what God requires from us. What He thinks should be more important than what man says. You need to come to a place in your relationship with God where you allow Him to remove the spirit of fear from over your life and fear Him.

Charm is deceitful and beauty is passing, But a woman who fears the Lord, she shall be praised. Proverbs 31:30

They were in right standing with God for their rebellion against what the evil Pharaoh plotted to do. *Exodus 1:21 tells us, "And so it was, because the midwives feared God that He provided households for them."* Their fearlessness of the king brought favour from the true King. God honoured them for the position they took and their households were provided for. What is also important to note is that their dauntless attitude helped in preserving a nation the enemy wanted to destroy.

The remarkable thing about fearing God is that, when you fear God, you fear nothing else; whereas, if you don't fear God, you fear everything else. – Oswald Chambers

Who or what is it that you fear? Is it God or man? When you have the fear of the Lord you need not worry about anything else. Fear of God provides security and protection from a life of ruin. The Word says to ask and it shall be given; how about asking God for the spirit of courage today when it comes to His statutes? Be like the midwives and when you see an injustice being done, stand against it and not with it.

Martin Luther spoke about servile fear and filial fear. A child usually fears his father; it's not the prison warden, inmate type of fear, but one of respect and honour to a person whom they love and admire. Filial fear is the type of fear that says I want to do the right thing because I don't want to displease you. It is the type of fear where when they are punished at times, they creep back into their father's arms after it is all over for his protection and further guidance. It is a fear that when Dad is around, they feel as though everything is right with the world and the biggest monster doesn't even scare them. That's what our fear of the Lord should look like.

A healthy fear of the Lord can be found in an attitude of awe, wonder, worship, and reverence. Let your passion, love and reverence of God drive you to civil disobedience if need be. Fear of the Lord will make you bold, strong, peaceful, and ready to do His will while fear of the enemy will make you weak and walk outside the will of God. Fearing God is one of the treasures you should and can gain as a woman who wants to grow in Him. So what will you choose?

And do not fear those who kill the body but cannot kill the soul. But rather fear Him who is able to destroy both soul and body in hell. Matthew 10:28

Chapter 8

A New Day is Dawning

"They stare as though they haven't seen me like this for years. You would think that everyone would be used to seeing the poor little lady with her bent back, but no, they still stare endlessly every day. After being stuck in this position for eighteen years, I am not certain anything can be done for me. My present isn't polite and my future isn't bright. My life consists of dirty roads, animal faeces and lots of feet. The pain never stops physically, but I try to suck it up and get on with my life. Today the pain is more intense than usual, but I will push through because I want to hear the teachings in the synagogue. It's going to be a rocky journey there, but I will press on." – *The Infirm Woman*

I recently preached a sermon at church under this title but with a different story. After deciding to release this book in October, I felt the need to speak to you about the number ten and its significance, and what it means for you. The number ten symbolizes the completion of a cycle, and then the beginning of something entirely new or a brand new cycle; a completed course of time or completeness in divine order. Here are a couple examples that are in the Bible: The Ten Commandments, the ten plagues, the ten "God said" which appears in the creation week of Genesis chapter 1. Additionally, they were ten virgins, ten lepers, ten talents, ten "I AM's" spoken by Jesus in the Gospel of John and the list goes on.

I decided to take it a bit further and research the flower for the tenth month and found out that it is the marigold. The marigold flower opens with the sun and is usually called the "herb of the sun." These flowers need lots of sun for any kind of development. Let us identify with this spiritually; we need the "Son" Jesus Christ to grow, and bring us into our new day. Just like the marigold, when the Son touches our lives we open up and bloom. There is a story in the gospel of John about the woman with the spirit of infirmity who was healed by Jesus and she was brought into a new cycle after suffering for many years.

Now He was teaching in one of the synagogues on the Sabbath. And behold, there was a woman who had a spirit of infirmity eighteen years, and was bent over and could in no way raise herself up. But when Jesus saw her, He called her to Him and said to her, "Woman, you are loosed from your infirmity." And He laid His hands on her, and immediately she was made straight, and glorified God. Luke 13:10-13

This woman had a spirit of infirmity for eighteen long and probably tiring years. She was crippled and it was impossible to raise herself up. Imagine the constant gazes and pity she endured from people. Her everyday living was affected by this infirmity and even doing the simplest of tasks would have been either impossible or it took a relatively long time to get it done. Day in and day out all she saw was the feet of people and not their faces. Her issue had her so weighed down that it was impossible to look up and see hope on the horizon. The things we take for granted are the things she would have done anything to see or do.

Have you ever felt like you were living in a vicious circle? Facing a situation for many years and it has you bent over to the point that your hope is beginning to falter? Your everyday living has been affected by this issue and you are barely surviving. Do you want to hear something? Jesus did not die for you just so that you can survive; He died so that you can live! Your spirit of infirmity does not have to be something physical; yes, some of you have been struggling with sickness for way too long, but there are cycles of poverty, unforgiveness, fear, pain, divorce, soul ties, stagnation.

You alone know what you have been dealing with and what needs to be broken off your life. God is here and He is eager to bring you into a new cycle of healing. The Scripture says "But" Jesus saw her. She was crippled, but Jesus saw her; she was burdened down, but Jesus saw her; she was in pain; but Jesus saw her. Whatever you are facing today, add the conjunction "but" to it and bring God into the mix.

One thing I admire about this account is the fact that when Jesus saw her she was in the synagogue. When ridden with an ailment or disability it always poses a challenge in some way, and more time is usually needed to do various tasks. Still, she did not let her infirmity stop her from going to hear from the Lord. Do not let your ailment stop you from being in the presence of the Lord. Make sure to seek Him in all the seasons of your life.

When Jesus saw her He was filled with compassion and called out to her. He touched her and she was made straight immediately. She received a 180 degree turnaround. Her healing was instantaneous, complete and undeniable. He did not half-heal or quarter-heal her, she was completely and immediately healed. The Lord wants to heal you completely; I don't care how long you have been dealing with this issue, it only takes one touch to be made straight.

Oh how sweet is the praise on our lips for a loving and gracious Father. When Jesus healed her, she glorified His name. Maybe she let out a shout, or maybe she danced around the synagogue; we will never know. What we do know is that she praised His name and it was rightfully done. She did not forget to show appreciation for the healing she received.

When God breaks the old cycle from off your life, I want you to try your hardest not to go back to what He will free you from. Do not be like a dog going back to his vomit. The marigold's odour and root hormones scare away many animals and insects from the garden, as well as kills nematodes in the soil. Upon your newness in God, you will have a scent so strong that it will keep the past at bay if only you will continue to keep firm in the Lord.

You want to grow and glow in His glory? Well there are some things that have to go. You cannot put new wine in old wine skins. God wants to do a new work in you and through you. He is not turning the page for a new chapter; He is turning the page in a new book for your life. Are you ready for God to break the cycle from over your life? You are going from the cycle of not being able to, to being able to. A new day has dawned and God wants to touch you like never before. Repeat these words from this song I wrote called "A New Day is Dawning" and let them resonate in your spirit. It says "A new day is dawning I believe, the water is stirring I believe. Healing is happening, deliverance is coming, strongholds are breaking, I believe."

Chapter 9

Arise Thou Woman of God

For if you remain completely silent at this time, relief and deliverance will arise for the Jews from another place, but you and your father's house will perish. Yet who knows whether you have come to the kingdom for such a time as this? Esther 4:14

"I was predestined according to Him before the foundations of the earth, placed here to fulfil a work which has already been done. Inside of me is trapped the ability to accomplish my purpose, and I am ready to unlock and activate the treasure that lies deep within. The king required a queen for his kingdom. Was it possible for a peasant girl to be transformed to royalty? I obtained favour in the sight of Hegai who took charge of the potential wives of the king. My identity was kept secret, for it was not yet the appointed time to reveal who I was.

I was lavished with oil and myrrh and many beauty regimens, being thoroughly prepared before I was allowed to go before the king. The day had come, the hour was near and I walked faithfully into my future. The king was pleased, the people were enthused and the royal crown was set upon my head.

Haman, my husband's right hand man, was roaring like a lion, seeking to destroy my people. A decree was set, sealed with the signet ring and plans were set for destruction. Mordecai lamented for our people and informed me of the treacherous plans of Haman the Agagite. He wanted me to go before the king to make supplication and plead before him for my people, but I made countless excuses. Why couldn't Mordecai understand that death would be pronounced to me if I decided to enter the inner courts without a charge?

The time had come for me to make a decision. It is either I continue to enjoy the comfort and pleasures of my surroundings, or get up and do what God had called me to do. The decision was made; there was only one thing to do. I was about to risk it all for the sake of my people. *– Esther*

Arise, for this matter is your responsibility. We also are with you. Be of good courage, and do it. Ezra 10:4

Mordecai asked Esther, "Who knows whether you have come to the kingdom for such a time as this?" My question to you is, "Do you know that you are here for such a time as this and that God wants to use you? But you have to make yourself available?"

It was not by chance that Queen Vashti was removed from the throne. It was a well orchestrated, God-ordained setup in order to make room for Esther. Was it by chance that Esther was picked out of all the young girls in Shunem? That was another divine appointment. God had a plan brewing behind the scenes to take effect in the near future. Esther was appointed and anointed to do the job and so are you.

Wherever God guides, He provides and resides. I know that deep within you know that God has called you to do some things but you have been taking a nap for a long time. IT IS TIME TO GET UP! What is stopping you from taking up the mantle and walking in purpose? Ask yourself this: "What is it that scares me so much that I have wilfully put myself in a comatose state?" Hear this. When Mordecai told Esther about Haman's plans to destroy their people and pleaded with her to go into the king, she was afraid. She was hesitant about going before her husband because of the fear of the outcome. Death was the punishment for going to the king without being called. Mordecai wasn't having none of her excuses and basically snapped her out of her fear.

"Don't even think for one second that if you refuse to help the people that relief won't come from somewhere else. This isn't about you or me, but it's about protecting a nation. God has sent you here for such a time as now to speak on behalf of us. So pull yourself together and do what you were placed here to do."

Well, he didn't say those exact words, but you get my point. Just like Mordecai did with Esther, I am about to do with you. God has called you and for some reason you keep walking in fear instead of rising up. If you don't do what God has called you to do, someone else will. Yes, He called you but we all have free will, and if you choose to not do it then He will find someone else. This is not the time to play around and throw your excuses at God. Recess is over; it's time to get to work.

After her talk with her uncle, she decided to arise and walk in purpose. She went into the king not knowing if she would come out alive but she did it anyway. What was required of her from God for His people was now more important than her fear and her excuses. Her boldness even in light of her fear brought her tremendous favour from the Lord.

Woman of God arise, it is time for you to take position. What you are about to walk into is greater than any fear you could have. Remember what I said before about getting rid of the spirit of fear and walking in the fear of the Lord. Do you not want to see the extraordinary things God wants to do with your life? You have not yet touched the tip of what

God has planned for you; there is much in store if only you decide to wake up.

Very often we sit and watch other people maximize their potential and fulfil their purpose and we sit by coveting, yearning to possess what they have, but we are too lazy. We always say we want a double portion of anointing but a double portion of anointing comes with a double portion of work. You must guard your potential from the spirit of slothfulness. As children of God, we're not placed here by accident, but by God's design, and it's up to us to be all that God intends us to be. Are you willing to risk it all for the sake of Christ and His kingdom?

"I have been waiting for you a mighty long time and it's only so much I can take. Time after time I have watched as you overslept without realising that time is passing by. I tapped you gently and even nudged you firmly, but you still slept as if my promptings didn't mean anything. Do they? I want to use you but are you willingly to leave your bed behind and run towards Me and your purpose? Are you? Seasons have changed, years have gone by and yet you stay the same. Are you that afraid of the unknown and Me that you refuse to get of bed to see, smell, and taste my goodness and all that can be if you just move? Arise and shine my daughter, your day is here yet again. Please don't miss it." – God

Chapter 10

The Pursuit Is On

66 **A** s a woman who wants to grow in God, your focus should be on pursuing His heart. Just as the deer pants after the water brooks so our soul should long after Him. I want to break down the pursuit of God in the stages of a relationship for better clarification and emphasis.

> **O God, You are my God; early will I seek You; My soul thirsts for You; My flesh longs for You In a dry and thirsty land Where there is no water. So I have looked for You in the sanctuary, To see Your power and Your glory. Because Your lovingkindness is better than life, My lips shall praise You. Thus I will bless You while I live; I will lift up my hands in Your name. My soul shall be satisfied as with marrow and fatness, And my mouth shall praise You with joyful lips. Psalm 63:1-5**

Dating - Seeking God

After the salvation process where God has sought after

you and you have answered the call, it is now your turn to seek Him. Your interaction with God does not end at salvation as many tend to believe, that is only where it begins. It is about seeking His face continuously. When you are in the beginning stages of a relationship, you are excited about getting to know and spending time with that person. That eagerness and passion is needed when it comes to your relationship with the Lord. Pursuing the heart of God is not about coming to church every time the church door opens. It is an authentic and pure relationship with God where you have a sense of desperation for fellowship with the One who saved you. He is not a priority; He is the priority.

But seek first the kingdom of God and His righteousness, and all these things shall be added to you. Matthew 6:33. Are you seeking God's face instead of seeking His hands? Are you interested in God or only what He can give? I heard someone once say "Sometimes you may seek out of desperation, other times out of desire, and other times out of discipline. But always seek Him." This is something we should all adhere to and live by.

Courting - Spending Time With God

It is impossible to be intimate with anyone you don't spend time with. If you want to know God intimately, you have to put in some time. We have become connected to everything but God. We are connected to Facebook, Instagram,

Twitter, Snapchat, television, work hobbies you name it. I would like you to do something for me, tally up the amount of time you take to do irrelevant things, and then you will find out how much time you have to spend with the Lord. Be reminded that the glory fell on Moses because he spent time with God. You want to be all glowed up like Moses was, but are you spending time with the Master? God's glory does not just fall on anyone.

Your connection has been re-opened through Christ restoring us back to the Father, but you keep refusing to take advantage. Newsflash: YOU SPEND TIME WITH WHO YOU LOVE. You get up and testify about how much you love the Lord, but behind closed doors you are not spending time with Him. What kind of relationship is that? How can you hear God if you are not spending time with Him? Stop panting and salivating over everything else but God.

Prayer & God's Word

How can we be intimate with God? By diving into His Word. Spending time in prayer and the word is vital to your growth. I heard someone once say, "Prayer and the Word of God are like two wings of a bird. Both are necessary if the bird is to fly." You cannot be a prayer warrior yet do not read your Bible, likewise, you cannot read your Bible and neglect prayer.

Prayer is not you going to God when you are in need, but it is earnestly and fervently conversing with the Father, all the while listening, hearing and understanding. The very breath you breathe is a gift from God; therefore, why are you not using it to communicate with Him? The sad reality is that many people know their pastor more than they know God, don't be one of them.

Marriage - Intimacy

It should be our mission to get intimate with God. He said to draw near to Him and he will draw near to us. Intimacy is usually hard to come by; it happens by choice and not by chance. It zealously searches out a deeper personal appreciation. If you want to become a doctor you spend time studying the books and practicing. You cannot wake up one day and decide to be a doctor and walk into a hospital caring for patients. It takes time to get there. Intimacy is not instantaneous, but it is cultivated over time. Stop treating God like a one-night stand.

The thing about God is that He does not reveal His secrets to strangers, only to those who know Him. Are you close enough for Him to reveal His secrets to you? It is very important for us to know God and His Word for ourselves; many Christians know of God but do not know Him personally for themselves.

Understand that you can lose intimacy if you stop spending time with a person. This is one of the reasons for many failed marriages. A neglected plant will not grow, nor will a neglected relationship grow in richness and depth. Do you remember how it felt when you fell in love? Certainly, no one has to tell a person to spend time with his or her spouse. They do it on their own free will and they have such fervour. No one should have to remind you to spend time with the Lord. You just do it out of a delight for Him.

Why Should I Pursue God?

Intimacy Births Purpose

A baby comes out of fellowship and intimacy naturally. Hence, if you want to know your purpose and give birth spiritually, you need to seek God. "He is the manufacturer and we are the product," as the late Myles Munroe often said. In order for us to know what He has placed us here to do, we have to go back to Him.

It Brings Death to Self

Intimacy with God brings the flesh under subjection. The poisonous things begin to fall away. Bad attitudes, pride, lust, unforgiveness, the things that bear no fruit. Good fruit is always visible as a result of an intimate relationship with God. Self is crucified and Christ is glorified.

To Know the Voice & Heart of God

It is very important that we know the voice of God. As sheep we ought to be in tune with the voice of the shepherd, or we will depend on the voice of self, others, or the enemy. You need the know heart of God. So, diligently seek Him in order to know what breaks His heart and what pleases Him. We miss the voice of God because we don't know what it sounds like. Why is that? Lack of intimacy. If He comes in a whisper you cannot hear because you are not close enough.

Confidence In God

David's confidence in God was tremendously strong, that no matter what he faced, he was sure that God would deliver him. A close relationship with God gives us confidence in Him and His Word. In the not so great times, we hold firm and strong in the Lord knowing that even though we are facing a harsh situation, He is in our corner; we do not have to worry or be afraid.

When I remember You on my bed, I meditate on You in the night watches. Because You have been my help, Therefore in the shadow of Your wings I will rejoice. My soul follows close behind You; Your right hand upholds me. Psalm 63:6-8

We have lost our way and forgotten our first love and as such, our focus has been shifted for a very long time. Our minds are on the things of the world and that's where our pursuit will be. We're seeking money, relationships, house, vehicles, and fame. What is it all worth in the end if our relationship with God is in shambles? You say growth and glow is what you want? Then seek the King.

"Come near to the holy men and women of the past and you will soon feel the heat of their desire after God. They mourned for him, they prayed and wrestled and sought for Him day and night, in season and out, and when they had found Him, the finding was all sweeter for the long seeking. Complacency is a deadly foe of all spiritual growth" A. W. Tozer - The pursuit of God.

"Oh Lord, I promise to pursue You vigorously; this is the last day of me making You an option. I will place You above all else as You should rightfully be. I am tired of this distant relationship and not being able to hear Your voice and not know what You want from me. You have been there all along, just waiting for me to take that step closer to You but I have been a rebel, what a shame. My hands are dirty of this accusation of a lacking relationship with You, but I promise to do better, I promise to try harder, and I promise to go deeper in You. I pray for my soul to follow close behind you, much like a child hanging on to its mother with a grip so tight that she is unable to go anywhere without

him. I have slipped up but Your forgiveness is sure, I have neglected You but Your love never left me. I have been playing in stagnant water for a really long time that I have collected numerous parasites, but You are the living water. It's You and me together; I know everything won't be a breeze, but I am confident that the growth and glow that I will obtain from Your glory will keep me grounded in You. So I thank you God, for what You are about to do in my life, this Girl and her God will set the world on fire." *–Your Daughter*

A Girl and Her God

May you pursue the God who pursued
You and took you out of the filth,
Clothing you in righteousness and giving
You the thousand cattle on the hill.
If you are separated from the King it
Means that you are the one who is running;
Baby girl, it's time to seek Him and get to glowing.

Arise and shine for your time has come,
Quit being stagnant and stop fooling around.
You are the Girl and He is your God,
It's time for you to grow so you can see His Glory flow.
— Shaniqua L. Howell

OTHER BOOKS
BY SHANIQUA L. HOWELL

#Diary Of A Girl

#DIARY of a Girl is not just another book about struggling through your singleness and how to overcome. This is the diary of a broken girl who became a Mighty Woman of God. The author, Shaniqua Howell, offers a deep, intuitive understanding to other single women concerning their relationships with men, their sexuality and the importance of waiting on God. In the process of this journey, you will laugh, weep and at times scream, as this book ministers to you.

The Waiting Room

The invitations were out and the date was written in stone for Sariah Parker's big day, but two months shy of her wedding God shook the very foundation of her plans and she was faced with more than she had bargained for. God had changed all the rules and instructed her to sever her relationship with her soon-to-be husband Justin Johnson and she was devastated. Back in the waiting room once again, she was gripped with the fear of running out of time and was completely overwhelmed about the status of her unknown future.

Life wasn't going as planned and she needed to face the truth quickly and make a decision that would alter her future forever. The cards were dealt and it was time for her to bluff or play straight; to be the loser or the winner, but the choice was all hers.

She might just receive more than she dreamed possible if only she would just walk in obedience. Will she choose to trust God and His plan or will she go about doing things on her own? Will she walk in blind faith knowing that God loves her enough to give her His best or will she forfeit everything God has in store for her life?

Confessions Of Scarred Souls

There is a type of broken only God can fix, and the women and men in this book can all attest to this. They possessed the spirit of an unbroken stallion, willful and determined to fight on no matter what they have been through. Understanding that every crisis contains seeds for transformation and growth, they turned their pain into power; their struggles into strength and their trauma into triumph. Scarred mentally, emotionally or physically, they had sworn off love and relationships forever. But through forgiveness, healing and restoration, they experienced a wholeness which could only be found in God. 'Confessions Of Scarred Souls' is a compilation of true stories of the tragedy of scarred and dark souls, to the triumph of a love that conquers all; the love of God. The valley never took them out; they somehow used the trials as a catapult to get them to their mountain top, their dark pasts never stopped them from having a bright future. These are their confessions!

A Girl and

Her G❀D

-Journal-

"When walking in the promises of God and you find yourself between a rock and a hard place, don't weep, rejoice! You're in good company for Jesus is the rock and Jesus is the strong tower." –Minister St Clair Browne

Dear God,

*Your Daughter*_____

The name of the LORD is a strong tower; the righteous run to it and are safe. Proverbs 18:10

"If we are to experience the revelation & manifestation of the Super natural power of Christ, we must be in relentless pursuit of the heart & mind of God." –Samuel Carter

Dear God,

 *Your Daughter_____*

And you will seek Me and find Me, when you search for Me with all your heart. Jeremiah 29:13

"Woman of God arise and dry your teary eyes. I have allowed you to be torn because I have anointed you to go before the king's throne. You were handpicked, moulded and purified, and for this reason, My chosen generation will not die. So get up, move...now is the time, for I am about to pour out new wine." —Malissa Craigg

Dear God,

 *Your Daughter*_____

Arise, for this matter is your responsibility. We also are with you. Be of good courage, and do it. Ezra 10:4

"My heart sings this song: "Through the fire, to the limit, to the wall… Through the fire, through whatever, come what may…" Lord! My trust is forever in You, My faith is all that stays." —Prophetess Nicole "Nicki" Welch

Dear God,

 Your Daughter_____

Behold, I have refined you, but not as silver; I have tested you in the furnace of affliction. Isaiah 48:10

"Never let your situation blind you of your two greatest resources - your faith and the close proximity of a God who responds to it." – Pastor Adrian Reid

Dear God,

*Your Daughter*_____

You will keep him in perfect peace, Whose mind is stayed on You, because he trusts in You. Isaiah 26:3

"God's love goes deeper and wider than we can ever fathom. Even in our filth, He still reaches down and lavishes His love on us. If that isn't love then I don't know what is." – Shaniqua L. Howell

Dear God,

 *Your Daughter*_____

Behold what manner of love the Father has bestowed on us, that we should be called children of God! Therefore the world does not know us, because it did not know Him. 1 John 3:1

"Rejection can mess up our psyche and alter our outlook on life. One way to combat rejection is to keep our eyes focused on Christ. He not only experienced it but He is our burden bearer. You cannot be resilient without the help of God. You want to snap back from rejection? Seek Jesus." – Theastarr Valerie

Dear God,

 *Your Daughter*_____

"Can a woman forget her nursing child, And not have compassion on the son of her womb? Surely they may forget, Yet I will not forget you." Isaiah 49:15

"Perhaps our greatest obstacle in understanding God's grace is having the perception that in some way we deserved it. If we could somehow make ourselves good enough then we wouldn't need God. When we accept how horrible we are and how great He is, then we can begin to fathom how wonderful His grace truly is." –Rev Michael Holford

Dear God,

 *Your Daughter*_____

Let us therefore come boldly to the throne of grace, that we may obtain mercy and find grace to help in time of need. Hebrews 4:16

"Naomi lost everything except her daughter in law. Her struggles did not go unnoticed because God, He saw. The Lord restored her with so much more when Boaz passed their way. When you put your trust in God, it will be the dawning of a new day." – Tamara Yearwood

Dear God,

 *Your Daughter*_____

And we know that all things work together for good to those who love God, to those who are the called according to His purpose. Romans 8:28

"A woman fears the Lord is more concerned with how He views her than the world. A woman who fears the Lord desires for the intentions of her heart to be seen. A woman who fears the Lord, her obedience will always be honoured. A woman who fears the Lord, possesses true strength, even if people may perceive her as a coward. A woman who fears the Lord seeks to please God above man. A woman who fears the Lord, upon solid ground, she will always be able to stand." – Kathilia Edghill

Dear God,

 *Your Daughter*_____

A Psalm of David. The Lord is my light and my salvation; Whom shall I fear? The Lord is the strength of my life; Of whom shall I be afraid? Psalm 27:1

*"It is well despite the trials I face, I know God is preparing me
to exhibit grace."* — Pastor Caldon Charles

Dear God,

 *Your Daughter*_____

*I will say of the Lord, "He is my refuge and my fortress;
My God, in Him I will trust." Psalm 91:2*

"Just as money is the currency of the earth, faith is the currency of the Kingdom of God. It is by faith we are able to draw on the eternal resources and promises of God. The scriptures say God provided all that pertains to life and godliness and by that we must understand that lack is never our portion. With a mentality of lack you focus on everything you don't have and you might even complain in vanity. With the understanding that God has already given you all that you need (past tense), that faith can be exercised in an all-powerful God to provide in times of need. How do we know that we truly have faith? The scriptures say that faith without works is dead, therefore believe God to what He says." – Raymond Thomas

Dear God,

 *Your Daughter_____*

That your faith should not be in the wisdom of men but in the power of God. 1 Corinthians 2:5

"The day is dawning in the east, with it comes the promise of joy, restoration and peace. But behold, closed dark thoughts at the windows of the soul, deceive many that the loving God has not answered our call." —Minister St Clair Browne

Dear God,

 *Your Daughter*_____

But You, O Lord, do not be far from Me;
O My Strength, hasten to help Me! Psalm 22:19

"A woman who fears the Lord is like a small pebble which is used by the Master builder to plug the hole of a leaking dam." – Malissa Craigg

Dear God,

 *Your Daughter_____*

Be strong and of good courage, do not fear nor be afraid of them; for the Lord your God, He is the One who goes with you. He will not leave you nor forsake you." Deuteronomy 31:6

"Our brokenness is not a signal that God has abandoned us if we are in His will. It is instead an opportunity to access God's grace and healing for our body, mind and soul. It is in this accessing that He is glorified as we are reminded that we are helpless without Him." —Rev Michael Holford

Dear God,

*Your Daughter*_____

You are my hiding place; You shall preserve me from trouble; You shall surround me with songs of deliverance. Selah Psalm 32:7

"What I have is little, it's not quite enough! You're the God of miracles, You're the God of signs and wonders, I stand on Who You are, So Increase me Lord. Show forth Thy power and Thy might." – Prophetess Nicole "Nicki" Welch

Dear God,

🌼 *Your Daughter*_____

But Jesus looked at them and said, "With men it is impossible, but not with God; for with God all things are possible." Mark 10:27

"In life, the child of God may experience times of passing through the fire. Fire does two main things; it either destroys or brings forth what is pure. Many times we can interpret the fire in our lives as fire to destroy us but we must be reminded according to Romans 8:28 and Jeremiah 29:11, if by no other way, that God's intent for us is never bad but for our best. With this in mind we must search deep within ourselves and think, what is God trying to burn away in my life? Or what is God bringing forth in me by allowing me through this fire? You'll come to find that like gold, fire brings out the purest in your spirit." — Raymond Thomas

Dear God,

 *Your Daughter*_____

That the genuineness of your faith, being much more precious than gold that perishes, though it is tested by fire, may be found to praise, honor, and glory at the revelation of Jesus Christ. 1 Peter 1:7

"You can come to God as a broken and empty vessel and watch Him fill you until you overflow and have some to share. He'll never leave you lonely or stranded, with faith in Him just listen and see He is always there." – Tamara Yearwood

Dear God,

 *Your Daughter_____*

Therefore may God give you Of the dew of heaven, Of the fatness of the earth, And plenty of grain and wine. Genesis 27:28

"But seek ye first the kingdom of God, and his righteousness; and all these things shall be added unto you." Matthew 6:33. "This verse of scripture has become so cliché that (some) believers say it just to sound pious. It has no connotation to them at all. However, Christ gave a formula and it is imperative that we follow through with God's command. Seeking God's Kingdom first is vital to our Christianity. When we take care of God's business, He takes care of ours." –Theastarr Valerie

Dear God,

 *Your Daughter* _____

Seek the Lord and His strength; Seek His face evermore! 1 Chronicles 16:11

"Our passion to succeed must outweigh the frustration of rejection for us to be successful." – Samuel Carter

Dear God,

 *Your Daughter*_____

For You formed my inward parts; You covered me in my mother's womb. I will praise You, for I am fearfully and wonderfully made; marvelous are Your works, and that my soul knows very well. Psalm 139:13-14

"Arise thou Woman of God, take up your mantle and remember your place. The sacred space the Lord has given to you, your job is to fill it and He will always set the pace. Your race is not for the quick, but for those who will hold fast and stick close to the Father's breast. Willing to risk it all and sacrifice whatever He says because you know He's got your best interest at heart, and He'll provide just who and what you need on your journey, every single part." – Kathilia Edghill

Dear God,

 *Your Daughter_____*

There are many plans in a man's heart, Nevertheless the Lord's counsel--that will stand. Proverbs 19:21

"There is a time and a season for everything under the sun. Some fruit in our life only grows well in the dark, hard and painful periods of our lives. But grow it does, and this fruit of our suffering not only nourish our own souls with new joy but it also gives life to many others." – Pastor Adrian Reid

Dear God,

 *Your Daughter_____*

But I have trusted in Your mercy; my heart shall rejoice in Your salvation. I will sing to the Lord, because He has dealt bountifully with me. Psalm 13:5-6

"It is well with me because God is my shield, so even in the times of distress and raging seas, I will trust my Lord because in Him I have the Victory." –Shaniqua L. Howell

Dear God,

 *Your Daughter*_____

Casting all your care upon Him, for He cares for you. 1 Peter 5:7

Dear God,

🌼 *Your Daughter*_____

Dear God,

🌼 *Your Daughter*_____

Dear God,

*Your Daughter*_____

Dear God,

✿ *Your Daughter*_____

Dear God,

🌼 *Your Daughter*_____

Dear God,

Your Daughter_____

Dear God,

Your Daughter_____

Dear God,

Your Daughter_____

Dear God,

*Your Daughter*_____

Dear God,

Your Daughter_____

Dear God,

✿ *Your Daughter*_____

Dear God,

🌼 Your Daughter_____

Dear God,

✿ *Your Daughter*_____

Dear God,

✿ Your Daughter_____

Dear God,

Your Daughter_____

Dear God,

🌼 Your Daughter_____

Dear God,

*Your Daughter*_____

Dear God,

✽ Your Daughter_____

Dear God,

✿ *Your Daughter*_____

Dear God,

🌼 *Your Daughter_____*

Dear God,

✿ *Your Daughter*_____

Dear God,

🌼 *Your Daughter*_____

Dear God,

🌼 *Your Daughter_____*

Dear God,

*Your Daughter*_____

Dear God,

Your Daughter_____

Dear God,

✿ Your Daughter_____

Dear God,

✿ *Your Daughter*_____

Dear God,

*Your Daughter*_____

Dear God,

*✿ Your Daughter*_____

Dear God,

🌼 *Your Daughter*_____

Dear God,

Your Daughter _____

Made in the USA
Monee, IL
27 April 2022

95545060R00085